Taco Fiesta
A Culinary Journey into the World of Tacos

TACO FIESTA

First edition. January 4, 2024.

Copyright © 2024 Jose Maria.

ISBN: 979-8224546695

Written by Jose Maria.

Table of Contents

Jose Maria

❖ Introduction

A. Brief history of tacos:

Tacos have a rich and diverse history, originating from the indigenous people of Mexico. The word "taco" is believed to have come from the silver mines in Mexico, where miners used to wrap gunpowder in pieces of paper and insert them into holes in the rock known as "tacos" before igniting them. Over time, this concept evolved into the delicious and versatile dish we know today.

Tacos gained popularity across Mexican communities and eventually spread worldwide. From humble beginnings, tacos have become a global phenomenon, adapted and embraced by various cultures.

B. Importance of tacos in various cultures:

Tacos are more than just a delicious food item; they hold cultural significance in many societies. In Mexico, they are a staple of street food culture, enjoyed by people from all walks of life. Tacos also play a significant role in celebrations and family gatherings, symbolizing unity and tradition.

Beyond Mexico, tacos have become a canvas for culinary creativity in numerous cultures. Whether it's the Korean BBQ taco, the Tex-Mex beef taco, or the Mediterranean lamb gyro taco, each adaptation reflects the unique flavors and traditions of its origin.

C. Overview of the cookbook:

Taco Fiesta: A Culinary Journey into the World of Tacos is a celebration of the diversity and versatility of tacos. This cookbook is designed to be a guide for both beginners and seasoned cooks, exploring traditional and innovative taco recipes.

The cookbook is organized into various sections, starting with the essentials of crafting the perfect taco, including a detailed exploration of ingredients, tools, and assembly tips. From there, readers will embark on a journey through classic tacos, regional variations, creative twists, vegetarian and vegan options, flavorful salsas and sauces, and even dessert tacos.

For those looking to host a taco-themed gathering, the book provides practical tips for setting up a taco bar, suggestions for beverage pairings, and overall advice for creating a memorable taco party experience.

In the conclusion, we'll recap the diverse taco varieties introduced in the cookbook and encourage readers to experiment, adapt, and create their own unique taco recipes. The appendix includes helpful conversion charts, a glossary of taco-related terms, and additional resources for further exploration. Get ready to embark on a flavorful adventure with Taco Fiesta!

Chapter (1) Taco Essentials

A. Ingredients:

1. Tortillas:

Tortillas are the foundation of any good taco. Choose from corn or flour tortillas based on personal preference or the type of taco you're making. If possible, warm them before serving for a more authentic and pliable texture.

2. Protein options:

Beef: Use thinly sliced sirloin for Carne Asada Tacos, ground beef for Tex-Mex Beef Tacos, or shredded beef for Birria Tacos.

Chicken: Grill chicken thighs for a smoky flavor in Chicken Street Tacos or use shredded rotisserie chicken for convenience.

Pork: Slow-cooked and shredded pork shoulder is perfect for Carnitas Tacos, while marinated pork works well for Al Pastor Tacos.

Fish: Choose a firm white fish like cod for Baja Fish Tacos. Coat in a light batter and fry until golden.

Vegetarian: Options include sautéed mushrooms, seasoned black beans, or grilled tofu for a satisfying meatless alternative.

3. Fresh vegetables and toppings:

Lettuce: Shredded iceberg or romaine lettuce adds a crisp texture.

Tomatoes: Diced tomatoes provide juiciness and freshness.

Onions: Finely chopped red or white onions add a sharp kick.

Cilantro: Fresh cilantro leaves contribute a burst of herbal flavor.

Avocado: Sliced or mashed avocado enhances creaminess.

Radishes: Thinly sliced radishes offer a peppery crunch.

4. Sauces and salsas:

Pico de Gallo: A fresh salsa made with tomatoes, onions, cilantro, jalapeños, and lime juice.

Guacamole: Mashed avocados mixed with diced tomatoes, onions, cilantro, lime juice, and salt.

Creamy Chipotle Sauce: Blend chipotle peppers in adobo with sour cream for a smoky and spicy sauce.

Mango Salsa: Dice ripe mangoes and mix with red onion, jalapeño, cilantro, and lime juice for a sweet and tangy salsa.

5. Cheese and garnishes:

Cheese: Crumbled queso fresco, shredded cheddar, or a Mexican cheese blend.

Garnishes: Lime wedges, hot sauce, and pickled jalapeños for personalized flavor adjustments.

B. Tools and equipment:

1. Taco press:

A taco press ensures uniformly thin and round tortillas. If you don't have one, a rolling pin works well for shaping the tortillas.

2. Griddle or skillet:

Use a griddle or skillet to warm tortillas and cook proteins. A cast-iron skillet is excellent for achieving a delicious sear.

3. Various kitchen utensils:

Tongs: Essential for flipping and handling hot proteins.

Spatula: Useful for flipping delicate fish or ensuring even cooking.

Knife and cutting board: For chopping vegetables and garnishes.

4. Tips for taco assembly:

Assemble fresh: To maintain texture, assemble tacos just before serving.

Layering: Start with the protein, add fresh ingredients, and finish with sauces and cheese.

Balance: Aim for a balance of flavors and textures in each taco.

With these essential ingredients and tools, you're ready to embark on a delicious taco-making adventure!

Chapter (2) Classic Tacos

A. Traditional Street Tacos
   1. Carne Asada Tacos:
Ingredients:

- **Thinly sliced sirloin steak**
- **Corn tortillas**
- **Fresh cilantro, chopped**
- **White onion, finely chopped**
- **Lime wedges**
- **Pico de Gallo**

Instructions:

1. Marinate the steak in a mixture of lime juice, garlic, cumin, and chili powder for at least 30 minutes.
2. Grill the steak over high heat until it reaches your desired doneness.
3. Warm the corn tortillas on the grill or in a dry skillet.
4. Assemble the tacos by placing slices of carne asada on the tortillas.
5. Top with chopped cilantro, finely chopped onions, and a squeeze of lime juice.
6. Serve with Pico de Gallo on the side.

2. Al Pastor Tacos:
Ingredients:

- **Marinated pork (thinly sliced or shredded)**
- **Pineapple chunks**
- **Corn tortillas**
- **Chopped onions and cilantro**
- **Creamy Chipotle Sauce**

Instructions:

1. Marinate the pork in a blend of dried chilies, achiote paste, pineapple juice, and spices for a few hours or overnight.
2. Cook the marinated pork on a grill or skillet until fully cooked and slightly caramelized.
3. Grill pineapple chunks until they get grill marks.
4. Warm the corn tortillas.
5. Assemble the tacos with the al pastor, grilled pineapple, and top with chopped onions and cilantro.
6. Drizzle with Creamy Chipotle Sauce.

3. Carnitas Tacos:
Ingredients:

- **Slow-cooked and shredded pork shoulder**
- **Corn tortillas**
- **Diced white onion and fresh cilantro**
- **Salsa verde**
- **Lime wedges**

Instructions:

1. Season the pork shoulder with cumin, oregano, garlic, and

orange juice. Slow-cook until tender.

2. Shred the pork and crisp it up on a skillet for added texture.
3. Warm the corn tortillas.
4. Assemble the tacos with the carnitas, diced onions, fresh cilantro, and a spoonful of salsa verde.
5. Serve with lime wedges on the side.

B. Regional Variations

1. Baja Fish Tacos:

Ingredients:

- **Battered and fried white fish (such as cod)**
- **Flour or corn tortillas**
- **Shredded cabbage**
- **Lime crema**
- **Baja Sauce**
- **Sliced radishes**

Instructions:

1. Coat the fish in a light batter and fry until golden brown.
2. Warm the tortillas.
3. Assemble the tacos with the fried fish, shredded cabbage, lime crema, and Baja Sauce.
4. Garnish with sliced radishes for a crunchy kick.

2. Tex-Mex Beef Tacos:

Ingredients:

- **Seasoned ground beef**
- **Flour tortillas**
- **Shredded lettuce**

- **Diced tomatoes**
- **Shredded cheddar cheese**
- **Sour cream**

Instructions:

1. Cook the seasoned ground beef until browned and fully cooked.
2. Warm the flour tortillas.
3. Assemble the tacos with the ground beef, shredded lettuce, diced tomatoes, shredded cheddar cheese, and a dollop of sour cream.

3. Yucatan Shrimp Tacos:
Ingredients:

- **Grilled or sautéed shrimp**
- **Corn tortillas**
- **Pickled red onions**
- **Mango salsa**
- **Avocado slices**

Instructions:

1. Grill or sauté shrimp until they are opaque.
2. Warm the corn tortillas.
3. Assemble the tacos with the shrimp, pickled red onions, mango salsa, and slices of avocado.
4. Serve with lime wedges on the side.

These classic and regional tacos are sure to transport you to the streets of Mexico and beyond. Enjoy the flavorful journey!

Chapter (3) Creative Twists on Tacos

A. Fusion Tacos

1. Korean BBQ Taco:

Ingredients:

- **Thinly sliced beef (bulgogi-style)**
- **Flour tortillas**
- **Kimchi**
- **Shredded lettuce**
- **Gochujang mayo**
- **Sesame seeds**

Instructions:

1. Marinate the beef in a mixture of soy sauce, brown sugar, garlic, and sesame oil. Grill or pan-cook until done.
2. Warm the flour tortillas.
3. Assemble the tacos with the Korean BBQ beef, kimchi, shredded lettuce, and a drizzle of gochujang mayo.
4. Garnish with sesame seeds for added crunch.

2. Mediterranean Lamb Gyro Tacos:

Ingredients:

- **Sliced lamb (marinated with Mediterranean spices)**
- **Pita bread or small flour tortillas**
- **Tzatziki sauce**
- **Chopped tomatoes**
- **Sliced red onions**
- **Fresh parsley**

Instructions:

1. Marinate the lamb in a mix of olive oil, garlic, oregano, and lemon juice. Grill or pan-cook until medium-rare.
2. Warm the pita bread or flour tortillas.
3. Assemble the tacos with the sliced lamb, tzatziki sauce, chopped tomatoes, sliced red onions, and a sprinkle of fresh parsley.

3. Thai Chicken Satay Tacos:
Ingredients:

- **Grilled chicken satay strips**
- **Small corn tortillas**
- **Peanut sauce**
- **Shredded cabbage**
- **Chopped peanuts**
- **Fresh cilantro**

Instructions:

1. Skewer and grill chicken strips marinated in a mixture of coconut milk, curry, and soy sauce.
2. Warm the small corn tortillas.
3. Assemble the tacos with the grilled chicken satay, drizzle with peanut sauce, shredded cabbage, chopped peanuts, and fresh cilantro.

B. Breakfast Tacos
1. Chorizo and Egg Tacos:
Ingredients:

- **Chorizo sausage, cooked and crumbled**
- **Scrambled eggs**
- **Small flour tortillas**

- **Shredded cheddar cheese**
- **Salsa or pico de gallo**
- **Fresh cilantro (optional)**

Instructions:

1. Cook chorizo until browned and crumbly. Scramble eggs separately.
2. Warm the small flour tortillas.
3. Assemble the tacos with chorizo, scrambled eggs, shredded cheddar cheese, and top with salsa or pico de gallo.
4. Garnish with fresh cilantro if desired.

2. Veggie Breakfast Tacos:
Ingredients:

- **Sautéed mushrooms, bell peppers, and onions**
- **Scrambled tofu or eggs (for a non-vegan version)**
- **Small corn tortillas**
- **Avocado slices**
- **Salsa verde**
- **Fresh cilantro**

Instructions:

1. Sauté mushrooms, bell peppers, and onions until tender. Scramble tofu or eggs separately.
2. Warm the small corn tortillas.
3. Assemble the tacos with the sautéed veggies, scrambled tofu or eggs, avocado slices, and top with salsa verde.
4. Garnish with fresh cilantro.

3. Huevos Rancheros Tacos:
Ingredients:

- **Fried or poached eggs**
- **Corn tortillas**
- **Refried beans**
- **Ranchero sauce**
- **Shredded Monterey Jack cheese**
- **Sliced jalapeños (optional)**

Instructions:

1. Prepare fried or poached eggs.
2. Warm the corn tortillas.
3. Assemble the tacos with a layer of refried beans, a fried or poached egg, drizzle with ranchero sauce, and sprinkle with shredded Monterey Jack cheese.
4. Add sliced jalapeños for an extra kick if desired.

These creative twists on tacos bring a global fusion of flavors to your table, whether it's for lunch, dinner, or even breakfast! Enjoy experimenting with these unique combinations.

Chapter (4) Vegetarian and Vegan Tacos

A. Grilled Veggie Tacos:
   Ingredients:

- Portobello mushrooms, sliced
- Zucchini, sliced
- Bell peppers, sliced
- Red onion, thinly sliced
- Corn tortillas
- Avocado slices
- Fresh cilantro
- Lime wedges
- Olive oil, for grilling
- Fajita seasoning

Instructions:

1. Toss sliced mushrooms, zucchini, bell peppers, and red onion in olive oil and fajita seasoning.
2. Grill the vegetables until they are tender and slightly charred.
3. Warm the corn tortillas.
4. Assemble the tacos with the grilled veggies, avocado slices, fresh cilantro, and a squeeze of lime juice.

B. Black Bean and Corn Tacos:
Ingredients:

- Canned black beans, drained and rinsed
- Corn kernels (fresh or frozen)
- Small flour tortillas
- Shredded lettuce
- Diced tomatoes

- **Salsa or pico de gallo**
- **Vegan sour cream**
- **Cilantro for garnish**

Instructions:

1. In a pan, heat black beans and corn until warmed through.
2. Warm the small flour tortillas.
3. Assemble the tacos with a layer of black beans and corn, shredded lettuce, diced tomatoes, salsa or pico de gallo, and a dollop of vegan sour cream.
4. Garnish with fresh cilantro.

C. Jackfruit Carnitas Tacos:
Ingredients:

- **Canned young green jackfruit in brine, drained and shredded**
- **Corn tortillas**
- **Red cabbage, thinly sliced**
- **Vegan chipotle mayo**
- **Lime wedges**
- **Fresh cilantro**
- **Cumin, smoked paprika, garlic powder for seasoning**

Instructions:

1. Sauté shredded jackfruit in a pan with cumin, smoked paprika, and garlic powder until it resembles pulled pork.
2. Warm the corn tortillas.
3. Assemble the tacos with the jackfruit, thinly sliced red cabbage, a drizzle of vegan chipotle mayo, and a squeeze of lime juice.
4. Garnish with fresh cilantro.

These vegetarian and vegan taco options are packed with flavor and offer a delicious alternative to traditional meat-based tacos. Enjoy the plant-powered goodness!

Chapter (5) Salsas and Sauces

A. Pico de Gallo:
   Ingredients:

- Tomatoes, diced
- White onion, finely chopped
- Fresh cilantro, chopped
- Jalapeño, finely chopped (seeds removed for milder version)
- Lime juice, to taste
- Salt and pepper, to taste

Instructions:

1. In a bowl, combine diced tomatoes, finely chopped white onion, cilantro, and jalapeño.
2. Squeeze lime juice over the mixture.
3. Season with salt and pepper to taste.
4. Stir well and let it sit for at least 15 minutes to allow the flavors to meld.
5. Serve as a fresh and vibrant topping for tacos.

B. Guacamole Variations:
Classic Guacamole:

- Ripe avocados, mashed
- Red onion, finely chopped
- Garlic, minced
- Lime juice
- Salt and pepper to taste

Tomato and Onion Guacamole:

- Classic guacamole ingredients

- **Tomato, diced**

Mango and Jalapeño Guacamole:

- **Classic guacamole ingredients**
- **Ripe mango, diced**
- **Jalapeño, finely chopped**

Instructions:

1. For each variation, mash ripe avocados in a bowl.
2. Add the respective ingredients for the chosen guacamole version.
3. Mix well, adjusting lime juice, salt, and pepper to taste.
4. Serve immediately with tortilla chips or as a topping for tacos.

C. Creamy Chipotle Sauce:
Ingredients:

- **Vegan mayonnaise or regular mayonnaise**
- **Adobo sauce from canned chipotle peppers**
- **Lime juice**
- **Garlic powder**
- **Salt, to taste**

Instructions:

1. In a bowl, combine mayonnaise, adobo sauce, lime juice, and garlic powder.
2. Stir until well combined.
3. Taste and add salt if needed.
4. Adjust the spiciness by adding more or less adobo sauce.
5. Refrigerate for at least 30 minutes before serving to enhance flavors.

6. Drizzle over tacos for a smoky and creamy kick.

D. Mango Salsa:
Ingredients:

- **Ripe mango, diced**
- **Red onion, finely chopped**
- **Fresh cilantro, chopped**
- **Jalapeño, finely chopped**
- **Lime juice**
- **Salt, to taste**

Instructions:

1. In a bowl, combine diced mango, finely chopped red onion, cilantro, and jalapeño.
2. Squeeze lime juice over the mixture.
3. Season with salt to taste.
4. Stir well and let it sit for at least 15 minutes to allow the flavors to meld.
5. Serve this sweet and tangy salsa alongside tacos for a refreshing contrast.

These salsas and sauces will add a burst of flavor to your tacos, allowing you to customize each bite to your liking. Enjoy the vibrant and zesty accompaniments!

Chapter (6) Taco Party Tips

A. Setting up a Taco Bar:

Tortilla Station:

Offer a variety of tortillas, including both corn and flour, to accommodate different preferences.

Keep tortillas warm in a cloth-lined basket or tortilla warmer.

Protein Options:

Set up a separate station for each protein, such as grilled chicken, carne asada, or black beans, with warmers to keep them hot.

Provide labels with protein names for easy identification.

Fresh Toppings:

Arrange bowls of fresh toppings like shredded lettuce, diced tomatoes, chopped onions, sliced radishes, and cilantro.

Include sliced avocados or guacamole for added creaminess.

Salsas and Sauces:

Display an array of salsas and sauces, including pico de gallo, guacamole variations, creamy chipotle sauce, and mango salsa.

Offer mild to spicy options to cater to different heat preferences.

Cheese and Garnishes:

Provide a selection of cheeses such as crumbled queso fresco, shredded cheddar, and a vegan cheese alternative.

Offer lime wedges, hot sauce, and pickled jalapeños as garnishes.

Accompaniments:

Include classic Mexican sides like rice and beans.

Offer bowls of corn chips or tortilla chips for scooping up extra toppings.

Taco Assembly Station:

Set up a designated area for assembling tacos with plates, napkins, and utensils.

Provide instructions or a sign with suggested taco layering for guests.

B. Cocktail and Beverage Pairings:

Margaritas:

Serve classic lime margaritas or experiment with fruit variations like mango or strawberry.

Include a non-alcoholic version for guests who prefer a refreshing mocktail.

Mexican Beers:

Offer a selection of Mexican beers such as Corona, Modelo, or Pacifico.

Create a beer station with lime wedges and salt for rimming glasses.

Tequila Shots:

Provide a tequila tasting station with a variety of tequilas for guests to sample.

Offer salt and lime slices for traditional tequila shots.

Aguas Frescas:

Prepare refreshing non-alcoholic agua frescas in flavors like hibiscus, tamarind, or cucumber.

Serve in large dispensers with ice for a cooling beverage option.

Sangria:

Offer a fruity and vibrant sangria with red or white wine, mixed fruits, and a splash of citrus.

C. Tips for Hosting a Taco-Themed Gathering:

Customization is Key:

Ensure there are options for various dietary preferences, including vegetarian and vegan choices.

Label ingredients and allergens to accommodate guests with dietary restrictions.

Create a Festive Atmosphere:

Use colorful tablecloths, banners, and Mexican-inspired decorations to set the mood.

Play lively mariachi or salsa music to enhance the festive ambiance.

Interactive Entertainment:

Set up a taco-making competition or a "best taco" voting station for added fun.

Provide recipe cards for guests to jot down their favorite taco creations.

Keep it Casual:

Encourage guests to mingle and serve themselves, embracing the casual and interactive nature of taco gatherings.

Consider using disposable plates and utensils for easy cleanup.

Plan Ahead:

Prepare as much as you can in advance to minimize stress on the day of the event.

Ensure there are enough serving utensils, napkins, and trash bins for easy access.

Communicate Dietary Information:

Clearly communicate any dietary information to guests in advance.

Include a list of ingredients for each dish on display.

Enjoy the Fiesta:

Don't forget to enjoy the party yourself! Engage with guests, taste different tacos, and savor the vibrant atmosphere.

Hosting a taco-themed gathering is not just about the food; it's about creating a lively and memorable experience for your guests. ¡Que aproveche! (Enjoy your meal!)

Chapter (7) Dessert Tacos

A. Churro Tacos:
Ingredients:

- **Small flour tortillas**
- **Vegetable oil, for frying**
- **Cinnamon sugar mixture**
- **Dulce de leche or chocolate sauce**
- **Vanilla ice cream**
- **Sliced strawberries (optional)**

Instructions:

1. Heat vegetable oil in a deep pan for frying.
2. Cut small circles from the flour tortillas using a cookie cutter.
3. Fry the tortilla circles until golden brown and crispy.
4. While still warm, coat each churro shell in the cinnamon sugar mixture.
5. Drizzle dulce de leche or chocolate sauce inside the churro shells.
6. Scoop a small scoop of vanilla ice cream into each shell.
7. Garnish with sliced strawberries if desired.
8. Serve immediately for a delightful churro taco experience.

B. Fruit-filled Dessert Tacos:
Ingredients:

- **Small corn tortillas**
- **Greek yogurt or coconut yogurt (for a vegan option)**
- **Assorted fresh fruits (berries, kiwi, mango, etc.)**
- **Honey or maple syrup**
- **Chopped nuts (such as almonds or pistachios)**

Instructions:

1. Warm the small corn tortillas.
2. Spread a layer of Greek yogurt or coconut yogurt on each tortilla.
3. Arrange a variety of fresh fruits on top of the yogurt.
4. Drizzle with honey or maple syrup for sweetness.
5. Sprinkle with chopped nuts for added crunch.
6. Fold the tortillas in half, creating a taco shape.
7. Serve these delightful fruit-filled dessert tacos for a light and refreshing treat.

C. Chocolate and Peanut Butter Tacos:
Ingredients:

- **Chocolate tortillas or regular tortillas dipped in melted chocolate**
- **Creamy peanut butter**
- **Sliced bananas**
- **Mini marshmallows**
- **Chopped peanuts**
- **Chocolate syrup**

Instructions:

1. Dip regular tortillas or use chocolate tortillas if available in melted chocolate.
2. Allow the chocolate-covered tortillas to cool and harden.
3. Spread a layer of creamy peanut butter on each chocolate tortilla.
4. Place slices of banana on top of the peanut butter.
5. Sprinkle mini marshmallows and chopped peanuts over the bananas.
6. Drizzle with chocolate syrup for an extra chocolatey touch.

7. Fold the tortillas in half to form a taco shape.
8. Indulge in the decadence of these chocolate and peanut butter tacos.

These dessert tacos offer a sweet conclusion to your taco-themed meal, providing a delightful twist on traditional flavors. Enjoy the sweetness of these creative taco-inspired desserts!

Chapter (8) Tantalizing Toppings

A. Pickled Red Onions:
Ingredients:

- **Red onions, thinly sliced**
- **White vinegar**
- **Water**
- **Sugar**
- **Salt**
- **Optional: whole black peppercorns, bay leaves**

Instructions:

1. In a saucepan, combine equal parts white vinegar and water.
2. Add sugar and salt to the mixture, adjusting to taste. For a standard ratio, start with 1 tablespoon of sugar and 1 teaspoon of salt per cup of liquid.
3. Optional: Add whole black peppercorns and bay leaves for added flavor.
4. Bring the mixture to a boil, stirring until sugar and salt are dissolved.
5. Place the thinly sliced red onions in a heatproof jar or bowl.
6. Pour the hot vinegar mixture over the onions, ensuring they are fully submerged.
7. Allow the pickled onions to cool to room temperature, then refrigerate for at least an hour before serving.
8. Use pickled red onions as a tangy and vibrant topping for tacos.

B. Cilantro Lime Crema:
Ingredients:

- **Sour cream or Greek yogurt**
- **Fresh cilantro, finely chopped**
- **Lime juice**
- **Garlic, minced**
- **Salt and pepper, to taste**

Instructions:

1. In a bowl, combine sour cream or Greek yogurt with finely chopped fresh cilantro.
2. Add lime juice, minced garlic, salt, and pepper to taste.
3. Mix well until all ingredients are evenly incorporated.
4. Adjust lime juice and salt according to your preferences.
5. Refrigerate the cilantro lime crema for at least 30 minutes before serving.
6. Spoon the crema generously over tacos for a creamy and zesty finish.

C. Spicy Jalapeño Slaw:
Ingredients:

- **Green cabbage, finely shredded**
- **Carrots, grated**
- **Jalapeños, thinly sliced (seeds removed for milder heat)**
- **Mayonnaise or Greek yogurt**
- **Apple cider vinegar**
- **Honey or agave syrup**
- **Cumin, ground**
- **Salt and pepper, to taste**

Instructions:

1. In a large bowl, combine finely shredded green cabbage, grated carrots, and thinly sliced jalapeños.

2. In a separate bowl, whisk together mayonnaise or Greek yogurt, apple cider vinegar, honey or agave syrup, ground cumin, salt, and pepper.
3. Pour the dressing over the cabbage mixture and toss until well coated.
4. Adjust seasoning and sweetness according to taste preferences.
5. Let the slaw sit in the refrigerator for at least 30 minutes to allow flavors to meld.
6. Spoon the spicy jalapeño slaw onto tacos for a crunchy and flavorful topping.

These tantalizing toppings add layers of flavor and texture to your tacos, enhancing the overall dining experience. Mix and match these toppings to create the perfect combination for your taste buds. Enjoy the culinary adventure!

Chapter (9) Regional Taco Specialties

A. Sonoran Hot Dogs:
  Ingredients:

- **Beef hot dogs**
- **Bacon slices**
- **Soft hot dog buns**
- **Pinto beans, mashed**
- **Diced tomatoes**
- **Diced onions**
- **Diced fresh jalapeños**
- **Mustard**
- **Mayonnaise**
- **Salsa verde**

Instructions:

1. Wrap each beef hot dog with a slice of bacon and secure with toothpicks.
2. Grill the bacon-wrapped hot dogs until the bacon is crispy and the hot dogs are cooked through.
3. Warm the soft hot dog buns on the grill or in a skillet.
4. Spread a layer of mashed pinto beans on the inside of each bun.
5. Place a bacon-wrapped hot dog in each bun.
6. Top with diced tomatoes, onions, and fresh jalapeños.
7. Drizzle with mustard, mayonnaise, and salsa verde.
8. Serve these Sonoran hot dogs for a unique and flavorful regional specialty.

B. Tijuana-style Tacos Gobernador:

Ingredients:

- **Large flour tortillas**
- **Shrimp, deveined and peeled**
- **White cheese (queso blanco or Monterey Jack), shredded**
- **Bell peppers, thinly sliced**
- **White onion, thinly sliced**
- **Olive oil**
- **Garlic, minced**
- **Cilantro, chopped**
- **Lime wedges**

Instructions:

1. In a skillet, heat olive oil and sauté minced garlic until fragrant.
2. Add shrimp to the skillet and cook until they turn pink and opaque.
3. Remove the shrimp from the skillet and set aside.
4. In the same skillet, add more oil if needed and sauté sliced bell peppers and onions until softened.
5. Lay a large flour tortilla on a flat surface.
6. Place a portion of the sautéed vegetables on one half of the tortilla.
7. Top with cooked shrimp and a generous amount of shredded white cheese.
8. Fold the tortilla in half, creating a half-moon shape.
9. Cook the taco on a griddle or skillet until the cheese is melted and the tortilla is golden.
10. Garnish with chopped cilantro and serve with lime wedges.

C. Oaxacan Tlayudas:
Ingredients:

- **Large corn tortillas (tlayudas)**
- **Refried black beans**
- **Oaxacan cheese or mozzarella, shredded**
- **Avocado, sliced**
- **Radishes, thinly sliced**
- **Shredded lettuce**
- **Salsa (mild or spicy)**
- **Mexican crema or sour cream**
- **Optional: Grilled or shredded chicken, beef, or pork**

Instructions:

1. Spread a layer of refried black beans on one side of a large corn tortilla.
2. Sprinkle a generous amount of shredded Oaxacan cheese or mozzarella over the beans.
3. Optional: Add grilled or shredded chicken, beef, or pork if desired.
4. Heat the tlayuda on a griddle or skillet until the cheese is melted and the tortilla is crisp.
5. Remove from heat and top with sliced avocado, radishes, shredded lettuce, and salsa.
6. Drizzle with Mexican crema or sour cream.
7. Fold the tlayuda in half and serve immediately.

These regional taco specialties capture the diverse and delicious flavors of different Mexican regions. Enjoy the unique twists and culinary traditions that each one brings to the table!

Chapter (10) Healthier Alternatives

A. Lettuce Wrap Tacos:
Ingredients:

- Large lettuce leaves (butter lettuce or iceberg)
- Lean ground turkey or chicken
- Taco seasoning
- Cherry tomatoes, halved
- Avocado, sliced
- Red onion, finely chopped
- Fresh cilantro, chopped
- Greek yogurt or salsa (for topping)

Instructions:

1. In a skillet, cook lean ground turkey or chicken with taco seasoning until fully cooked.
2. Wash and dry large lettuce leaves, using them as taco shells.
3. Spoon the cooked meat onto each lettuce leaf.
4. Top with halved cherry tomatoes, sliced avocado, chopped red onion, and fresh cilantro.
5. Drizzle with Greek yogurt or salsa for added flavor.
6. Roll or fold the lettuce leaves to create a taco shape.
7. Enjoy these lettuce wrap tacos as a lighter, carb-conscious option.

B. Cauliflower and Chickpea Tacos:
Ingredients:

- Cauliflower florets
- Canned chickpeas, drained and rinsed
- Olive oil
- Taco seasoning
- Small corn tortillas
- Shredded cabbage or slaw mix
- Lime wedges
- Avocado, sliced
- Fresh cilantro, chopped

Instructions:

1. Toss cauliflower florets and chickpeas in olive oil and taco seasoning.
2. Roast in the oven until cauliflower is tender and chickpeas are crispy.
3. Warm small corn tortillas.
4. Assemble the tacos with the roasted cauliflower and chickpeas.
5. Top with shredded cabbage or slaw mix, lime wedges, sliced avocado, and chopped fresh cilantro.
6. Serve these cauliflower and chickpea tacos for a plant-based alternative.

C. Quinoa and Black Bean Tacos:
Ingredients:

- **Quinoa, cooked**
- **Canned black beans, drained and rinsed**
- **Corn tortillas**
- **Salsa verde or your favorite salsa**
- **Shredded lettuce**
- **Diced tomatoes**
- **Red onion, finely chopped**
- **Fresh cilantro, chopped**
- **Lime wedges**

Instructions:

1. Cook quinoa according to package instructions.
2. Warm corn tortillas.
3. In a bowl, mix cooked quinoa and black beans.
4. Spoon the quinoa and black bean mixture onto each tortilla.
5. Top with salsa verde, shredded lettuce, diced tomatoes, chopped red onion, and fresh cilantro.
6. Squeeze lime wedges over the tacos for a burst of citrus flavor.
7. Enjoy these quinoa and black bean tacos as a nutritious and satisfying option.

These healthier taco alternatives offer a variety of flavors and textures while incorporating nutrient-dense ingredients. Feel free to customize these recipes to suit your dietary preferences and enjoy guilt-free taco goodness!

Chapter (11) Kids' Corner

A. Miniature Taco Bites:

Ingredients:

- Mini taco shells or tortilla cups
- Ground beef or turkey, seasoned with taco seasoning
- Shredded cheddar cheese
- Cherry tomatoes, diced
- Sour cream
- Sliced black olives (optional)
- Chopped green onions (optional)

Instructions:

1. Prepare mini taco shells or use tortilla cups.
2. Brown ground beef or turkey in a skillet and season with taco seasoning.
3. Spoon the seasoned meat into each mini taco shell.
4. Top with shredded cheddar cheese, diced cherry tomatoes, a dollop of sour cream, and any optional toppings like sliced black olives or chopped green onions.
5. Arrange these miniature taco bites on a platter for a fun and bite-sized taco experience.

B. Cheesy Taco Quesadillas:

Ingredients:

- Flour tortillas
- Shredded cheddar cheese
- Ground beef or turkey, seasoned with taco seasoning
- Diced tomatoes
- Mild salsa (optional)

Instructions:

1. In a skillet, cook ground beef or turkey and season with taco seasoning.
2. Place a flour tortilla on a griddle or skillet over medium heat.
3. Sprinkle shredded cheddar cheese over half of the tortilla.
4. Spoon the seasoned meat and diced tomatoes over the cheese.
5. Fold the tortilla in half, creating a quesadilla.
6. Cook until the cheese is melted and the tortilla is golden brown on both sides.
7. Optional: Serve with mild salsa for dipping.
8. Allow the quesadillas to cool slightly before slicing into kid-friendly wedges.

C. DIY Taco Pockets:
Ingredients:

- **Large flour tortillas**
- **Cooked and shredded chicken or beef**
- **Refried beans**
- **Shredded lettuce**
- **Diced tomatoes**
- **Shredded cheddar cheese**
- **Sour cream**
- **Guacamole or sliced avocados**

Instructions:

1. Lay out large flour tortillas on a flat surface.
2. In the center of each tortilla, create an assembly line of ingredients, including shredded chicken or beef, refried beans, shredded lettuce, diced tomatoes, shredded cheddar cheese, sour cream, and guacamole or sliced avocados.
3. Allow kids to fill their own taco pockets with their favorite ingredients.
4. To create the pocket, fold in the sides of the tortilla and then fold up the bottom, creating a sealed pocket.
5. Secure the pocket with toothpicks if needed.
6. Kids can enjoy their DIY taco pockets with minimal mess and lots of fun!

These kid-friendly taco recipes are designed to be interactive, tasty, and just the right size for little hands. Enjoy creating a playful and enjoyable dining experience for the younger taco enthusiasts!

Chapter (12) Taco-inspired Beverages

A. Margaritas and Variations:
Classic Margarita:

- Tequila
- Triple sec
- Fresh lime juice
- Simple syrup
- Ice

Fruit Margarita:

- Tequila
- Triple sec
- Fresh fruit puree (strawberry, mango, or watermelon)
- Fresh lime juice
- Simple syrup
- Ice

Spicy Jalapeño Margarita:

- Tequila
- Triple sec
- Fresh lime juice
- Jalapeño slices
- Agave syrup
- Tajín seasoning for rimming glasses
- Ice

Instructions:

1. For each margarita variation, combine the ingredients in a shaker with ice.
2. Shake well and strain into glasses rimmed with salt or Tajín seasoning.
3. Garnish with lime wedges or fruit slices.
4. Enjoy these refreshing margaritas as the perfect accompaniment to your taco feast.

B. Agua Frescas:

Watermelon Agua Fresca:

- **Fresh watermelon, cubed**
- **Water**
- **Lime juice**
- **Agave syrup or sugar to taste**
- **Ice**

Cucumber Mint Agua Fresca:

- **Fresh cucumber, sliced**
- **Fresh mint leaves**
- **Water**
- **Lime juice**
- **Agave syrup or sugar to taste**
- **Ice**

Pineapple Basil Agua Fresca:

- **Fresh pineapple, chopped**
- **Fresh basil leaves**
- **Water**
- **Lime juice**
- **Agave syrup or sugar to taste**
- **Ice**

Instructions:

1. Blend the fresh fruit or vegetables with water, lime juice, and agave syrup or sugar until smooth.
2. Strain the mixture to remove any pulp.
3. Serve over ice in glasses.
4. Garnish with additional fruit slices or herbs.
5. Agua frescas offer a light and hydrating beverage option for your taco-inspired meal.

C. Horchata Smoothies:
Ingredients:

- **Horchata (store-bought or homemade)**
- **Vanilla ice cream or frozen yogurt**
- **Cinnamon**
- **Banana**
- **Ice cubes**

Instructions:

1. In a blender, combine horchata, a scoop of vanilla ice cream or frozen yogurt, a banana, and a sprinkle of cinnamon.
2. Add ice cubes for thickness and blend until smooth.
3. Pour the horchata smoothies into glasses.
4. Garnish with a dusting of cinnamon on top.
5. Sip on these creamy and flavorful horchata smoothies alongside your tacos.

These taco-inspired beverages provide a range of flavors from classic and refreshing to fruity and spicy. Elevate your taco experience with these delightful drink options!

Chapter (13) The Art of Taco Presentation

A. Plating Techniques:
Stacked Tacos:

- Place three or four tacos on a plate, slightly overlapping.
- Stack them in a way that showcases the layers of ingredients.
- Drizzle sauces or salsas in between the tacos for added visual appeal.

Open-faced Tacos:

- Lay tortillas flat on the plate.
- Spread ingredients across the tortillas, allowing each topping to be visible.
- This technique works well for showcasing vibrant colors and textures.

Taco Trio:

- Arrange a trio of tacos in a row on a long plate.
- Vary the toppings on each taco for a visually dynamic presentation.
- This technique works particularly well for showcasing different taco varieties.

B. Colorful Garnishes:
Rainbow of Fresh Vegetables:

- Use a variety of colorful vegetables as garnishes.
- Include diced tomatoes, sliced radishes, vibrant bell peppers, and shredded purple cabbage.
- Arrange the vegetables in a visually pleasing pattern on top of the tacos.

Avocado Roses:

- Slice avocados thinly and fan them out in a circular pattern to resemble a rose.
- Place the avocado rose as a central garnish on top of a taco.
- This adds an elegant touch and a creamy element to the presentation.

Herb Sprinkles:

- Finely chop fresh herbs like cilantro, parsley, or chives.
- Sprinkle the chopped herbs on top of the tacos for a burst of color and flavor.
- This technique works well with tacos featuring lighter-colored ingredients.

C. Edible Flower Arrangements:
Floral Taco Toppings:

- Incorporate edible flowers like nasturtiums, pansies, or marigold petals as taco toppings.
- Place the edible flowers strategically on top of the tacos for a visually stunning presentation.
- Ensure the flowers are safe for consumption and pesticide-free.

Flower Cup Centerpiece:

- Create small cups or bowls made of edible flowers.
- Fill these cups with salsas, sauces, or guacamole.
- Arrange the flower cups in the center of the taco platter as a beautiful and functional centerpiece.

Herb-infused Water:

- Infuse water with edible flowers and herbs for a refreshing beverage option.
- Serve the herb-infused water in clear glasses or carafes alongside the taco spread.
- This adds a touch of sophistication to the overall presentation.

Remember, the art of taco presentation is about creating an inviting and visually appealing spread that enhances the dining experience. Get creative, play with colors, and let your artistic side shine as you present your delicious tacos in style!

Chapter (14) Historical Tacos

A. Aztec-era Tacos:

Background:

The origin of tacos can be traced back to indigenous Mexican cultures, including the Aztecs. While the term "taco" wasn't used, the concept of wrapping food in a flatbread-like vessel dates back to this era.

Ingredients:

- Thin maize tortillas
- Grilled or stewed meats (venison, turkey, or fish)
- Locally available vegetables and herbs
- Chili peppers

Preparation:

1. Aztecs used thin maize tortillas as a vessel to hold a variety of fillings.
2. Meats, such as venison or turkey, were cooked with local spices and herbs.
3. Vegetables like avocados, tomatoes, and chilies were commonly used as toppings.
4. The taco-like dish was a versatile and portable way to enjoy a balanced meal.

B. Evolution of Tacos in the U.S.:
Late 19th Century:

- Tacos first appeared in the United States in the late 19th century when Mexican migrants brought their culinary traditions with them.
- The first known English-language mention of tacos appeared in a cookbook in 1905.

Mid-20th Century:

- In the mid-20th century, tacos gained popularity in the U.S. with the rise of fast food.
- Glen Bell opened the first Taco Bell in 1962, introducing hard-shell tacos to a broader American audience.
- Tex-Mex cuisine, which includes taco variations, became increasingly popular.

Modern Era:

- Today, tacos are a staple in American cuisine, enjoyed in various forms, from street tacos to gourmet creations.
- The U.S. has embraced a wide range of taco styles, incorporating diverse ingredients and flavors.

C. Notable Taco Moments in History:
Taco Trucks and Street Food:
The rise of taco trucks and street food in the late 20th century played a significant role in popularizing authentic and diverse taco offerings.

National Taco Day:
National Taco Day is celebrated on October 4th in the United States, highlighting the cultural significance and widespread love for tacos.

Social Media Influence:
The influence of social media has played a crucial role in showcasing creative and visually appealing taco creations, contributing to the ongoing evolution of taco culture.

Tacos in Space:
In 2021, a shipment of tacos was sent to the International Space Station as part of a promotional collaboration between a tortilla brand and a space tourism company.

Tacos have not only evolved over centuries but have also become a global phenomenon, transcending cultural boundaries and finding a place in the hearts and palates of people around the world.

Chapter (15) DIY Tortilla Making

A. Corn Tortillas from Scratch:
Ingredients:

- **Masa harina (corn flour)**
- **Warm water**
- **Pinch of salt**

Instructions:

1. In a bowl, combine masa harina and a pinch of salt.
2. Gradually add warm water and knead the dough until it reaches a smooth consistency.
3. Divide the dough into golf ball-sized portions.
4. Use a tortilla press or roll out each ball into a thin, round tortilla.
5. Cook the tortillas on a hot griddle or skillet for about 30 seconds on each side until they puff slightly.
6. Keep warm in a clean kitchen towel until ready to serve.

B. Flour Tortillas with a Twist:
Ingredients:

- **All-purpose flour**
- **Baking powder**
- **Salt**
- **Warm water**
- **Olive oil or vegetable shortening**

Instructions:

1. In a bowl, mix all-purpose flour, baking powder, and salt.
2. Gradually add warm water and olive oil or vegetable shortening, kneading until the dough is smooth.
3. Divide the dough into golf ball-sized portions.
4. Roll out each ball into a thin, round tortilla using a rolling pin.
5. Cook on a hot griddle or skillet for about 30 seconds on each side until golden brown spots appear.
6. Stack the tortillas and keep them covered to stay warm.

C. Unique Tortilla Alternatives:

Spinach Tortillas:

Add pureed spinach to the flour and water mixture in your tortilla recipe for vibrant green spinach tortillas.

Sweet Potato Tortillas:

Incorporate mashed sweet potatoes into your tortilla dough for a subtly sweet and colorful alternative.

Chipotle-flavored Tortillas:

Mix ground chipotle powder or pureed chipotle peppers into your masa harina or flour tortilla dough for a smoky and spicy kick.

Turmeric and Cumin Tortillas:

Add ground turmeric and cumin to your flour tortilla dough for a warm and aromatic flavor profile.

Instructions (for Unique Alternatives):

1. Adjust the base tortilla recipe (corn or flour) according to the unique twist you want to incorporate.
2. Follow the steps for making traditional tortillas with the added ingredients.

Making tortillas from scratch allows you to customize the flavors and experiment with unique variations. Whether you choose traditional corn tortillas or get creative with unique alternatives, the process of DIY tortilla making adds a special touch to your taco experience.

Chapter (16) Global Taco Tour

A. Indian-inspired Curry Tacos:

Ingredients:

- **Roti or naan bread (as taco shells)**
- **Curry-spiced chicken or paneer**
- **Yogurt-based raita sauce**
- **Mango chutney**
- **Sliced cucumbers**
- **Chopped cilantro**

Instructions:

1. Grill or warm roti or naan bread to use as taco shells.
2. Season chicken or paneer with curry spices and grill or cook until fully cooked.
3. Fill each taco with the curry-spiced protein.
4. Top with a dollop of yogurt-based raita sauce.
5. Drizzle with mango chutney for sweetness.
6. Add sliced cucumbers for freshness and chopped cilantro for a burst of flavor.
7. Enjoy these Indian-inspired curry tacos with a fusion of aromatic spices.

B. French-inspired Ratatouille Tacos:

Ingredients:

- **Small flour tortillas**
- **Ratatouille (zucchini, eggplant, bell peppers, tomatoes, onions, garlic)**
- **Goat cheese or feta**
- **Balsamic reduction**

- **Fresh basil leaves**

Instructions:

1. Warm small flour tortillas.
2. Spoon ratatouille onto each tortilla.
3. Crumble goat cheese or feta on top.
4. Drizzle with balsamic reduction for a touch of acidity.
5. Garnish with fresh basil leaves.
6. Fold the tortillas for a French-inspired twist on tacos.
7. Enjoy the melding of Mediterranean flavors in these ratatouille tacos.

C. Moroccan-inspired Lamb Tacos:
Ingredients:

- **Pita bread (as taco shells)**
- **Ground lamb, seasoned with Moroccan spices**
- **Tzatziki sauce**
- **Harissa sauce**
- **Shredded lettuce**
- **Sliced tomatoes**
- **Crumbled feta cheese**

Instructions:

1. Toast or warm pita bread to use as taco shells.
2. Cook ground lamb with Moroccan spices until browned and flavorful.
3. Fill each pita taco with the seasoned lamb.
4. Drizzle with tzatziki sauce for creaminess.
5. Add a touch of harissa sauce for heat.
6. Top with shredded lettuce and sliced tomatoes.
7. Finish with crumbled feta cheese for a tangy accent.

8. Savor the rich flavors of these Moroccan-inspired lamb tacos.

Embark on a global taco tour with these diverse and internationally inspired taco recipes. Explore the fusion of flavors from different cuisines while maintaining the beloved taco format.

Chapter (17) Taco Challenges

A. Spicy Taco Challenge:
Ingredients:

- Spicy hot peppers or hot sauce of varying heat levels
- Jalapeños, habaneros, or ghost peppers
- Spicy salsa or hot chili powder
- Ground beef, chicken, or beans (as the taco filling)
- Tortillas

Instructions:

1. Create a range of spicy fillings using hot peppers or hot sauces of different heat levels.
2. Prepare tacos with varying degrees of spiciness, from mild to extremely hot.
3. Challenge participants to eat the spiciest tacos without taking a drink for a set period.
4. Have cooling elements like sour cream or yogurt on hand for participants to use if needed.
5. Consider keeping a "Spice Level Chart" to track participants' progress and spice tolerance.

B. Giant Taco Challenge:
Ingredients:

- Extra-large tortillas
- Double or triple portions of traditional taco fillings
- Exotic or unique taco toppings
- Salsa or hot sauces for extra flavor

Instructions:

1. Prepare giant tortillas by either purchasing oversized ones or combining several regular-sized tortillas.
2. Create massive portions of classic taco fillings such as seasoned meats, beans, and vegetables.
3. Add unique and adventurous toppings to make the giant taco visually appealing.
4. Challenge participants to finish the entire giant taco within a set time limit.
5. Encourage creativity in presentation for an entertaining and Instagram-worthy challenge.

C. Taco Eating Contest Tips:
Prepare Varied Fillings:
Offer a variety of taco fillings to cater to different preferences and dietary restrictions.
Establish Clear Rules:
Clearly communicate the rules, including the duration of the contest, acceptable eating techniques, and any penalties for rule violations.
Safety First:
Ensure that participants are aware of the spice levels, especially in spicy taco challenges, and have access to water or other beverages.

Use a Timer:
Keep track of the time to determine the winner accurately.
Celebrate the Winner:
Acknowledge and celebrate the winner with a prize, certificate, or social media recognition.
Encourage Spectator Participation:
Involve the audience by allowing them to cheer for their favorite participants or offering prizes for the best spectator signs.

Capture the Moment:

Document the taco challenge with photos or videos to share on social media, creating lasting memories and potential promotional content.

Remember to prioritize safety and enjoyment for participants and spectators alike when organizing taco challenges. These challenges can be a fun way to engage the community and showcase the love for tacos in a lively and entertaining manner.

Chapter (18) Tacos for Every Season

A. Summer Grilled Tacos:
   Ingredients:

- **Grilled chicken or shrimp**
- **Fresh pineapple chunks**
- **Avocado slices**
- **Red onion, thinly sliced**
- **Cilantro, chopped**
- **Lime wedges**
- **Corn tortillas**

Instructions:

1. Grill chicken or shrimp until fully cooked.
2. Grill pineapple chunks for a sweet and smoky flavor.
3. Assemble tacos with grilled protein, pineapple, avocado slices, red onion, and chopped cilantro on corn tortillas.
4. Squeeze lime wedges over the tacos for a burst of citrus freshness.
5. Enjoy these summer grilled tacos with a perfect balance of savory, sweet, and tangy flavors.

B. Fall Harvest Tacos:
Ingredients:

- **Roasted butternut squash or sweet potatoes**
- **Ground turkey or pork seasoned with fall spices (cinnamon, nutmeg, and cloves)**
- **Cranberry salsa**
- **Pomegranate seeds**
- **Goat cheese or feta**

- **Flour or corn tortillas**

Instructions:

1. Roast butternut squash or sweet potatoes until tender and slightly caramelized.
2. Cook ground turkey or pork with fall spices until browned and flavorful.
3. Assemble tacos with roasted squash or sweet potatoes, seasoned meat, cranberry salsa, pomegranate seeds, and crumbled goat cheese or feta on flour or corn tortillas.
4. Experience the autumn flavors in these fall harvest tacos.

C. Winter Comfort Tacos:
Ingredients:

- **Braised short ribs or shredded beef**
- **Caramelized onions**
- **Roasted Brussels sprouts**
- **Gorgonzola or blue cheese**
- **Red wine reduction sauce**
- **Flour tortillas**

Instructions:

1. Braise short ribs or slow-cook shredded beef until tender.
2. Caramelize onions for sweetness and depth of flavor.
3. Roast Brussels sprouts until golden and crispy.

Assemble tacos with the braised or shredded beef, caramelized onions, roasted Brussels sprouts, crumbled Gorgonzola or blue cheese, and drizzle with a red wine reduction sauce on flour tortillas.

Enjoy these winter comfort tacos with rich and hearty ingredients.

These seasonally inspired tacos capture the essence of each season, incorporating fresh and flavorful ingredients that complement the time of the year. Whether it's the smokiness of summer grilling, the warmth of fall spices, or the comforting flavors of winter, these tacos are sure to delight your taste buds throughout the year.

Chapter (19) Taco Leftovers Reinvented

A. Taco Salad Remix:
Ingredients:

- Leftover taco meat (beef, chicken, or vegetarian)
- Shredded lettuce
- Cherry tomatoes, halved
- Black beans, drained and rinsed
- Corn kernels
- Avocado slices
- Shredded cheese
- Tortilla strips
- Cilantro, chopped
- Salsa or dressing of choice

Instructions:

1. In a large bowl, combine shredded lettuce, cherry tomatoes, black beans, corn, and avocado slices.
2. Add leftover taco meat to the salad.
3. Top with shredded cheese and tortilla strips for crunch.
4. Garnish with chopped cilantro.
5. Drizzle with salsa or your favorite dressing.
6. Toss the salad to mix all ingredients thoroughly.
7. Enjoy a refreshing taco salad remix with the flavors of your favorite tacos.

B. Taco Pizza:
Ingredients:

- **Pre-made pizza dough or crust**
- **Refried beans**
- **Taco-seasoned ground beef or chicken**
- **Shredded Mexican cheese blend**
- **Diced tomatoes**
- **Sliced black olives**
- **Jalapeño slices**
- **Sour cream (for drizzling)**
- **Fresh cilantro, chopped**

Instructions:

1. Preheat your oven according to the pizza dough instructions.
2. Roll out the pizza dough onto a pizza stone or baking sheet.
3. Spread a layer of refried beans over the dough.
4. Top with taco-seasoned ground beef or chicken and shredded cheese.
5. Add diced tomatoes, sliced black olives, and jalapeño slices as toppings.
6. Bake according to the pizza dough instructions until the crust is golden and the cheese is melted.
7. Drizzle with sour cream and sprinkle with fresh chopped cilantro before serving.
8. Slice and enjoy a taco-inspired pizza twist.

C. Taco Stuffed Bell Peppers:
Ingredients:

- **Bell peppers, halved and seeds removed**
- **Leftover taco meat (beef, chicken, or vegetarian)**
- **Cooked rice**
- **Black beans, drained and rinsed**
- **Corn kernels**
- **Diced tomatoes**
- **Shredded cheese**
- **Taco seasoning**
- **Fresh cilantro, chopped**
- **Sour cream (optional)**

Instructions:

1. Preheat the oven to 375°F (190°C).
2. In a bowl, mix the leftover taco meat with cooked rice, black beans, corn, diced tomatoes, shredded cheese, and taco seasoning.
3. Stuff the halved bell peppers with the taco mixture.
4. Place the stuffed peppers in a baking dish.
5. Bake in the preheated oven for about 25-30 minutes or until the peppers are tender.
6. Garnish with fresh chopped cilantro and, if desired, a dollop of sour cream.
7. Serve these taco-stuffed bell peppers as a reinvented and nutritious meal.

These creative reinventions of taco leftovers showcase the versatility of taco components, offering new and exciting ways to enjoy the flavors you love. Whether it's a refreshing taco salad, a pizza with a taco twist, or stuffed bell peppers, these recipes add a delightful spin to your leftover taco ingredients.

Chapter (20) Tacos on the Go

A. Portable Taco Cones:
   Ingredients:

- **Small flour tortillas**
- **Grilled chicken, beef, or vegetarian taco filling**
- **Shredded lettuce**
- **Diced tomatoes**
- **Shredded cheese**
- **Sour cream**
- **Guacamole or sliced avocados**

Instructions:

1. Warm small flour tortillas.
2. Assemble taco cones by placing a portion of grilled taco filling on each tortilla.
3. Top with shredded lettuce, diced tomatoes, shredded cheese, sour cream, and guacamole.
4. Carefully roll the tortilla into a cone shape, securing it with a toothpick if needed.
5. Pack the portable taco cones in parchment paper or foil for a mess-free on-the-go meal.
6. Enjoy a convenient and flavorful taco experience wherever you are.

B. Taco-Inspired Wraps:
Ingredients:

- **Large tortillas (flour or whole wheat)**
- **Taco-seasoned meat or beans**
- **Salsa or pico de gallo**
- **Shredded lettuce**
- **Diced onions**
- **Shredded cheese**
- **Sour cream or Greek yogurt**
- **Cilantro, chopped**

Instructions:

1. Lay out large tortillas on a flat surface.
2. Spread a layer of taco-seasoned meat or beans onto each tortilla.
3. Top with salsa or pico de gallo, shredded lettuce, diced onions, shredded cheese, and a dollop of sour cream or Greek yogurt.
4. Sprinkle chopped cilantro over the toppings.
5. Fold in the sides of the tortilla and roll it up tightly, creating a wrap.
6. Secure the wrap with parchment paper or foil for a mess-free and portable taco-inspired meal.
7. These wraps are perfect for a quick and satisfying lunch on the go.

C. Freezer-friendly Make-Ahead Tacos:
Ingredients:

- Taco-seasoned meat or beans
- Small tortillas (corn or flour)
- Shredded cheese
- Salsa or pico de gallo
- Guacamole or sliced avocados
- Lime wedges (for squeezing before serving)

Instructions:

1. Cook taco-seasoned meat or beans according to your preference.
2. Allow the taco filling to cool completely.
3. Assemble small tacos by placing a spoonful of taco filling on each tortilla.
4. Top with shredded cheese, salsa or pico de gallo, and guacamole or sliced avocados.
5. Roll each taco and wrap them individually in plastic wrap.
6. Place the wrapped tacos in a freezer-safe bag and store in the freezer.
7. When ready to eat, reheat the frozen tacos in the microwave or oven.
8. Squeeze fresh lime wedges over the tacos before serving.
9. These make-ahead tacos are perfect for busy days or a quick freezer-friendly meal option.

These on-the-go taco variations provide convenient and mess-free ways to enjoy your favorite flavors wherever your day takes you. Whether it's a portable taco cone, a taco-inspired wrap, or freezer-friendly make-ahead tacos, these recipes are perfect for busy schedules and adventurous eaters.

❖ Conclusion

A. Recap of Taco Varieties:

In this culinary journey through the world of tacos, we've explored a diverse array of taco varieties that span traditional, creative, and globally inspired options. From classic street tacos like Carne Asada and Al Pastor to fusion creations like Korean BBQ and Thai Chicken Satay Tacos, each recipe brings its own unique flavors and cultural influences. We've ventured into breakfast tacos, vegetarian and vegan options, tantalizing salsas and sauces, and even indulged in dessert tacos. Whether you're hosting a taco party, seeking healthier alternatives, or exploring regional specialties, the possibilities are endless. Tacos truly offer a canvas for culinary creativity and a delightful experience for your taste buds.

B. Encouragement for Readers to Experiment and Create Their Own Taco Recipes:

As we conclude this taco-filled journey, I encourage you, the reader, to embark on your own taco adventures. Tacos are a versatile and customizable dish, allowing you to experiment with flavors, textures, and ingredients. Feel free to mix and match proteins, toppings, and sauces to create your signature tacos. Don't be afraid to infuse your cultural influences or try unexpected combinations. The joy of tacos lies in the exploration and personalization of this beloved dish. So, gather your favorite ingredients, unleash your culinary creativity, and savor the satisfaction of crafting unique and delicious tacos that reflect your tastes and preferences.

May your taco creations be a source of joy, shared moments, and culinary delight. Happy taco crafting!